Playing in Overtime
Poems

Copyright © 2025 by Barry Wallenstein
All Rights Reserved.
Printed in the United States of America
FIRST EDITION
Requests for permissions or to reprint or reuse material from this work
should be sent to:
The Ridgeway Press
c/o M. L. Liebler
5057 Woodward Avenue-9th Floor
Wayne State University
Detroit, MI 48202
Cover art and design: Carol McDonald
Designed and typeset by Brandon Wade
ISBN: 978-1-56439-083-7
Library of Congress Control Number: 2025934115
First Edition: 2025

Playing in Overtime
Poems

Barry Wallenstein

Detroit, MI

Also by Barry Wallenstein

BOOKS

Odd Men Out (or In), Xanadu Press, 2025
It's About Time, NYQ Books, 2022
Time on the Move, Xanadu Press, 2020
At the Surprise Hotel, Ridgeway Press, 2016
Tony's Blues Franck Berthoux with Pourquoi viens-tu si tard ? Éditions 02/20 Marilyne Bertoncini, trans.
Drastic Dislocations: New and Selected Poems, New York Quarterly Books, 2012
Tony's World, Birch Brook Press, 2009
A Measure of Conduct, Ridgeway Press, 1999
The Short Life of the Five-Minute Dancer, Ridgeway Press, 1993
Love and Crush, N.Y. Persea Books, 1991
Roller Coaster Kid, N.Y.: T.Y. Crowell, 1982
Beast Is A Wolf With Brown Fire, Brockport, N.Y.: BOA Editions, 1977
Visions and Revisions: An Approach to Poetry. N.Y.: T.Y. Crowell, 1971

RECORDINGS

Lisbon Sunrise, Sintoma Records, 2022
Lisbon Sunset, Sintoma Records, 2016
What Was, Was, Audioscope LC 12366, 2015
Lucky These Days, Cadence Jazz Records CJR 1242, 2013
Euphoria Ripens, Cadence Jazz Records CJR 1210, 2008
Pandemonium, Cadence Jazz Records CJR 1194, 2005
Tony's Blues, Cadence Jazz Records CJR 1124, 2001
In Case You Missed It, SkyBlue Records, CD # 106, 1995
Taking Off, AK-BA Records, #1040, 1982 LP [Reissued by Bleu Regard, France,
CT 1950, 1995]
Beast Is, AK-BA Records, #10200, 1978 L

Acknowledgments

Some of these poems first appeared in the following journals:

Manhattan Review
Plant-Human Connection Quarterly
Home Planet News
Live Mag
BigCityLit
Verse Daily
The Brownstone Poets Anthology, 2021& 2024
Unsinkable: Poetry Inspired by the Titanic (Anthology)

Special thanks to Barbara Rosenthal for her photographs and publication of my chapbook, *Odd Men Out (or In)* Xanadu Press 2/25

To Maya, the light of our days & nights

Contents

Persons of Interest 1
    At Home in a Tree 3
    The Waiting Man 4
    The Impatient Man 5
    A Questionable Man 6
    Raking 7
    At the Bar 8
    "Boy, 6, Found Wandering Drunk" 9
    The Tantrum 10
    Tony To His Pot Plant 11
    Sim Asks Sam 13
    The Man from Depressionville 14
    Ice Cold Murder 15
    Lamp Lights on Their Posts 16
    The I Am Variations 17

Intimacy 19
    To Lorena Sandra 21
    A Quick Stab at Lost 22
    In the Middle of the Story 23
    The Carnal Life 24
    Carnal Life 2 25
    Narcissus Distracted 26
    Inosculation 27
    Music Poem 28
    The Octogenarian Club Welcomes My Kid Brother 29
    Gratitude 30
    Song for Maya 31

    Fathers 32

    Father/Daughter 33

    Maya at 4 34

    Granddaughters 35

The Daily News **37**

    What Is 39

    Wartime 40

    Straus Park Memorial 41

    Wartime Blues 42

    Charlie's in Danger 43

    Folly 44

    The Chief 45

    The Chief, Still Without a Name 46

    Cancel Culture 47

    Tidal Pools 48

    The Sea Speaks to the Sand 49

Playing in Overtime **51**

    Survivor 53

    Last Leaf 54

    His November 55

    Pantoum for the Moment 56

    Companion 57

    A Fluky Fall 58

    Penultimate Words 59

    Speedo 60

    The Speed of a Bullet 61

    An Escape 62

    Recollection 63

First Responder 64
Grim Reaper 65
As of Late, It's Still Early 66
The Race 67
"Hereafter" 68
Lost and Found 69

Persons of Interest

At Home in a Tree

The man's found a cozy way to be
be it in a cell, a cave, a squat
or more lately,
the hollow of a giant plane tree
nestled in a bluff,
appointed with a utility kitchen
and a narrow cot off to the side –
a secure nest protected
against the tempests, tornados,
or violent downpours
that hurl hail stones.

If the weather calms,
he'll crawl from his covering,
conjure company, electricity, windows,
and once outside he'll chuckle a bit
to witness the population cavorting.
He'll find a cluster to talk to,
then gesture towards his tree
surrounded by hillocks,
smaller trees, and lilies.

The new friends follow him home
straight into the hollow
where they stoop to enter.
After some time, the tallest visitor leaves
and runs through the wood,
agile as a gazelle.
He retrieves something
and dashes back with it,
and crouches to re-join the party.

The Waiting Man

Not large enough to loom
he hovers.
Not small enough to disappear
He's here.

It's not the waiting that chafes,
but the fade from notice
and being caught —
tight faced or pouting,
insulted by the air he breathes
with no ready whip of anger
or target at which to strike.

Unmoving, frozen outside the door
behind which the committee sits,
he worries -- how to behave
when faced with rebuke
or that blasé look
ahead of the group's decision.

The Impatient Man

One day, on the verge of joy,
with everything promised
but not yet delivered,
he grew petulant.
It was as if certainty,
a visible jewel, not yet polished,
had fallen under a table
too far for retrieval.

So, he glowered and scuttled sideways,
all along shaking his head *no* –
as if this might convince someone
to pay attention
to the fidgety hands, lips slit red
and barely there.
Finally, with a self-conscious slant
to his script he scribbled "I quit."
However, he didn't quit;
he lingered in a scowl.

A Questionable Man

Even a slippery eel has a history
but this character is vapors;
he doesn't emanate from clouds—
he *is* clouds—plural.

When he plays cards,
he practices fear;
he prays, "Please, no picture cards,"
while sitting with a handful of aces.

As a baby, he sucked at his father's tit
and it was bitter, gall and wormwood.
Since then, things have been
a little bit better—

Mother passed too,
but mother's love remains,
soft and forgiving
while he is stuck, holding his aces.

Raking

For days, the sun burns down
onto the still green acre,
as Tommy forces his rake through the hay,
as Tommy forgets he's a boy – just 8 -
but conjures the great farmers,
Demeter, Cronus, and other imagined creatures,
and eagles – birds of prey to whom he prays,
birds that peck on wood
until they become wooden, petrified birds.

The spindly boy rakes and rakes
the cut grass into small piles,
then bunches them into one.
He tightens the bale with his body
and heaves the hefty cube
onto the wagon as the sun goes down.

Again, no shade for Tommy the next day
as he rakes in the distant field.
The sweat glows on the boy's face.
No one knows why he loves raking so,
or why he doesn't look up to see
his parents gazing from a window.
From where they sit, the rake
might be a sickle, or a scythe,
and their boy could be a farmer.

At the Bar

Jake the barkeep turns his back,
cuts his hooch with water,
then hires his friend Jack,
a lawyer, to hand it over –
a small man   with degrees
from certified universities,
who when he assists at bars,
it's to talk about the law
or the latest sensation in golf
or the fluctuations of the market.

Jack's in service to both the bars,
but tonight, he's thinking ahead
to the years beyond retirement,
when, if he were to buy his own bar,
he just might fall in with the need
to thin his gin, cut his rye to swell his luck.
Every gesture tried in daylight
would delight his friends.
Closing hours, he's out back
wearing faux leather trousers,
not much parlance, this sly little guy.

"Boy, 6, Found Wandering Drunk"

What collection of discordant notes
led the child to leave his home
so tanked up and wobbly
that the veins colored his eyes.
By the time he was picked up,
his baby blues were squeezed in a squint.

Had someone yelled *stupid!*
go back to where…or get out?
The police arrived, clicked their tongues,
and peppered the boy with questions:
who left the liquor cabinet open,
how long were you left alone?

Now that he's home,
the ones who love him
hold him tightly in his sleep.
One touches his hot calm face,
while the other brushes his swollen lip.

The Tantrum

The china bowl rimmed with a floral frieze,
preserved by 18th century glaze
sits beside a cut glass vase
on an ebony table
covered by a brocaded cloth,

but the boy's fisted anger
seeks this precious elegance
as his strong arms flail out
and blast the bowl and the vase;
the cloth is in bloody shreds.

His fury is temporary
while he proves all objects,
no matter how well placed,
are as transient
as the witnesses.

Tony To His Pot Plant

I've lifted off with a smile
and want nothing in return.
Oh, your feathery-green leaves,
your pistils, your flowers –
flourishing glory!

These sap-filled stems,
the cola coated in floral cluster,
drawn in over measured years,
have led to levitation.
From on high your cupping buds
have become my transport.

But I confess, dear common weed,
blooming marvel,
on some smoke-infused days,
my vision turns inward,
veers downward and I pause
to listen to your language
coded on waves I'd like to break.

Plant talks back:

"I'm medicinal, not cynical.
Ride your highs and your lows;
you're entitled to drift,
relax your frame,
and spend some time inside
your dream machine,
with its strobe-like enhancers,
to conjure the connections
between yourself and you
and the sacred life of my florets
and pistils. You filled your pipe
above the verdant valley.
Your gait proves my presence
in the tokes taken.

My fan leaves, my sugar leaves,
coated as they are,
wave to you, treasured smoker."

Sim Asks Sam

do you like Andrew?
        why not? he's here
        and never bothered anyone I know.
        His shirt's tucked in neat and clean,
and his breath's not foul
so no – I don't dislike Andrew *or* his randy laughter.

do you like Tony?
        it's too soon to tell;
        he's traveling – gone maybe to the moon.
        When he was here last
        he said nothing definitive.
        He's away.

and what about Sally?
        ah that one! the physical person and the idea.
        If only we could meet,
        share an edge of sand and the sight of
        the sea going out or coming in,
        then I'd know better.
Sam, Tony's been back a week now,
and he and Sally have been playing cards;
he's winning again and quiet as night.
How do you feel about that?

Sim, you control the questions
and often go beyond.
I answer them as best I can –
half the truth is half-way there.

The Man from Depressionville

One individual,
poorly shod and biting hard against his luck,
turned his desperation into action.

In the middle of March,
broke and wearing a mask,
he points his 45 magnum pistola
at a huddling group of bank tellers –
"hand over the high numbers
and look at me all the while steady
and believe me – one wrong move
and nobody gets outta here alive."

The film cliches slipped from his lips,
and a jolt of shame
sent a shiver down his shoulder
and into his heels and beyond the bank.
Soon, his gun hand dropped its weight.
The sudden clatter released the chatter
held in all those anxious faces.

Slowly, some calm returned,
and the lines reassembled.
Tellers returned to their tasks
not quite certain the danger was over
or how to regard the man –
bent low and crestfallen in retreat.

Ice Cold Murder
    after Agatha Christie

It was around 5 a.m.,
in an uptown section of Toledo,
when the icicle pushed its way
into Antonio's heart
where it stopped
and started to melt.

The shaft at last did liquefy,
and by then the pooling water
showed only flickering candle-lights.

As Antonio passed
his murderer slipped away,
hands already dry,
in the direction of the hotel Bye-N-Bye,
where in the back of the kitchen
he sculpts ice angels
with tiny brides and grooms,
their blank faces set atop his frosty display.

Lamp Lights on Their Posts

He envies the lamp lights,
loves their illumination,
their arcane circuitry,
their current accuracy,
static and size,
their separations post to post,
their triumphs in the rain,
and even their stuttering flickers.

He could chatter on,
if not seized by
a beautiful nakedness:
the lamppost: tall, curved atop,
fluted from the base
all the distance up to the crown
and fixed solid in the ground,
the pavement or motorway.

Such grace could stop a car,
and wouldn't the group be lucky
to get out alive, just scared
and with a story to tell
and sorrowful bills to pay.
The post itself will not buckle
and the number of posts is reassuring.

He'd copy the lamplight
if he could – send out a glow –
shed light on the flowers
and the bleeding deer.

The I Am Variations

I'm an old engine waiting
for a shot of oil,
a lubricant that's smooth, thick,
dark, and viscous enough
to slather my pistons so
they'll suffer no friction
driving me home.

I am the hungry mite chewing on daisies;
and the yellow in the middle, the petals too
compose my day.
No mild butterfly am I
though they too suck
and cause some local trauma.
We occupy the same territory.

I am lassitude itself, last on the list,
lolling about in a ring,
drifting with a license—to be
my father, long underground;
I am him and my children well-fed –
all the family, the living and dead.

Intimacy

To Lorena Sandra

Rabbits run to rabbit's care,
paw to paw crease to crease,
while you annihilate my sullen moods
and lead me to my animal side.
I burrow in furrows
for the salty glide,
clamber up tree trunks
for the succulent reds,
trace the marks where your rhythm tread.

So it goes and well into winter,
a tiger in town and me a twister,
a sweet-toothed monster
in love with a dancer and at times
her rising pulse. Slow me down –
I mean yes, if you need to –
and I'll fall in step with your rhythm if I can,
but put down your fan, your grip on the duende,
read my verses and hold my hand.

A Quick Stab at Lost

In the small room – a monk's cell –
poorly lit for a higher purpose,
she signed with her mouth
that she was lost.

Then I knew there were two of us
lost in such a tangled spell
we'd need a map, a trusted compass,
and the help of a wizard,
to navigate our separate ways back home;
and once there we'd each need amnesia
and millions of feathers to cushion the fall.

In the Middle of the Story

A young man in his twenties
is walking toward a city,
having made love for the last time
with his first sweetheart
who whispered at the open door
"No more. I enjoyed what was,
your tenderness, our trembles,
but that **magic** moment has passed."

The writing hand,
on its way to expressing
an ephemeral truth,
is shaken by an earth tremor.
By chance no one was hurt,
but the pen skidded on the paper
and the truth,
sincerely put forth, flew off.

The Carnal Life

Too few were the decades
of working the blood pressure,
shuffling the rules,
misremembering each other's names.

The first time – alone and then not –
fiercely into it, now later,
decades later,
fewer thrills, less soil.

The memory bank is flush and scarlet;
the week ahead is blank and dull
but for a date with the Gonad twins,
cousins of Onan, holder of the crown jewels.

Carnal Life 2

Smack me a kiss – quick
before I do it myself.
Plant your roses right here
before I abuse myself further
in front of you – or in that beveled mirror
behind you. I'd leave this ache behind
if, led by affection, the old-fashioned
getting-to-know-you, prevails.

We – if you can imagine
two small letters composing a we,
a date, a place to be in,
an hour in which to play
shy, but please,
be shy in my mouth, osculate.

Narcissus Distracted

Passing by a mirror,
he pays no attention
and gazes in the other direction.
He walks on without looking back.
It's enough to know I'm there he thinks.
Placing one small thought behind another,
he banishes envy, spite, rancor
and courts a breeze on its way
across a field of clover.

Well below the field,
beyond an opening in the fence,
the stream is damned,
and the water is pooled
cold and clear enough
to see down to the pebbles.
He breaks the surface
and counts the stones.

Inosculation[1]

In the semi-darkness,
I think I hear the sucking sounds
from trees merging in the woods.
I discover two maples – joined.
The smaller of the two
was cut and scarred years ago,
so the larger one has been holding it
and feeding it ever since.

This pair, grown together, sharing
the same sun-greened sugars,
the same nitrogen sucked up
from the roots. Is it fatuous to think
of wood in love, affection in bark –
the sweet sap?
I blanch at this exposed intimacy
unavailable to my kind.

They go to sleep together in autumn
and wake up together in spring.

---

[1] The Inosculation Process "The term is derived from the Latin roots in + ōsculārī, to kiss into/inward/against…; trees having undergone the process are referred to in forestry as gemels, from the Latin word meaning a pair."

Music Poem

It's your turn to bring in the dollars,
your turn to bring in the bread.
I refrain,
my back's nearly broke;
besides, there's been enough such carrying
in memory's cup to overflow the brim.

So think of my pockets as stitched
and me, former king of the cash machine,
out of town.

Last week it was your turn
to take out the smoke;
now it's my turn to bury the dollars
found in the yard
while searching back then
for arable land to plow.

Now it's this week again
and your turn to carry the cash,
my turn to blow out the smoke.
If we keep going this way,
who won't want to know us,
get close to us – marry us.

The Octogenarian Club Welcomes My Kid Brother
   for David at 80

It's taken you a good long while
to get here
all that time early on – playing
then working overtime
with some time off for sports,
island hopping and working again.

But Time's not the only theme.
There are also the faces of love:
your one love and
sometimes your boss;
and then your progeny
prompting more love in all directions.

So, though this club of seasoned players
is less populous than those
for the middle aged
much much less crowded than
the kiddie clubs – fun as they were,
joyfulness continues – and lately,
celebrations – let the revels persist!

Gratitude

Thanks Mom & Dad
for your tumble in the hay,
the tremble and release
that hit the spot and made my days.

Invisible presences now,
still potent and otherworldly,
locked in the vapors
I can barely see through.

Song for Maya

Maya turns two
and I *could* say boo hoo
for one
was so much fun
swinging on a swing
ridding on a donkey
holding nana & pop pop's hands
while walka walka walka
nice long naps/ the comfort of a pacifier
and every taste a new taste
all the way to two.

But now I say hooray!
for the two-year-old
is also the one-year-old
with added time tagged on
every day every day.
Already you point and say
what's that what's that
and the question mark
is clear and sharp
and you file away
each answer
even as you go out to play.

Now that you're two
there is so much to do:
running, jumping, spinning, singing –
and talking talking talking
and thinking thinking
and loving loving loving.

Fathers

Foolish is the father
not to fear and madly love
his son, well-armed, tall,
muscular and gripped by anger
with a hair-line trigger.

Lacking his howitzer,
if contradicted,
he'll employ a penknife
showing off an accurate thrust.
Some fathers would fall out of love.
This one could not,
and when the son is absent from himself
the dad too goes missing.
He searches streets and alleyways
for creation myths, flood stories.

This father chastens himself
in the final chapters
of his condition
as he confuses his son's anger
with his foolish own.

Father/Daughter

What do you write about
my sweet heart child
grown up like a flower
in your father's yard?

Sex & death, plentiful in the hills
steaming in the valleys –
that's all I bother with, my poppa.

Then why hide the pages
written in the dark
my blue eyed,
straight backed daughter?

>	Because you've taught me well
>	about the elves who snoop and tattle
>	while caught in your spell.

I have no spell, no spell at all,
and my elves adore your posture.
they rest in the hills, the protective hills
and no harm will come from them ever.

>	What you say makes me smile,
>	but I'll write my stories, dark and spicy
>	and give little thought to your shadow

I'll thin my shadow
clear to the ground
and turn my eyes from your pen,
my thoughts from your direction.

Poppa – smile, you'd have the last lines,
but the composition's mine –
you pine, you elm in the woods.

Maya at 4

Opens every door
and not just to our hearts –
the front door (now that I'm so tall)
and the back door (I'm very strong),
and the pantry door
for a snatched delight.

Boredom, ennui,
the mask of indifference
are nowhere beneath her curls.
Instead, her smile prompts
a universe of smiles
except for a fleeting scowl
or pout – on the way out.

The villains who dot the earth
are canceled by her culture
and maybe soon by her will
years before she knows it.

Now to the birthday song:
Maya Maya
you set our hearts on fire
and all the dreams you inspire
will come true
as four becomes you.

Granddaughters

Deep in the wee hours
she's a well of tears,
and her crying swamps
the angel minutes of her day
and challenges my concentration.
on the one perfect diamond
resting on a square of black glass.

This has been forever.
I've left my fascination hours ago.

Her eyes are slit creases,
her mouth a pink oval of noise:
or is this a grievance to disturb
even the neighbors at this hour?
I say no, don't relax into her sounds,
don't desire rest,
don't be that selfish.

The whole round world is riotous
with the old clanging of swords.
The new generation of arms
weighs on the scales
of her terrible wailing.

The Daily News

What Is

What is this day but an allowance
to go wild or calm down.
The actors act like clowns,
while the surrounding trees
burn from the inside out for lack of reason.
The reasonable crustaceans
know where to hide.

What is this music but a refuge from
the clatter of arms
and deafening certainties,
where even faith fails
within the tunnels, as listeners cluster
to avoid enormous shifts
in the tectonic plates.

What is this ocean but a lot of water
that touches on seashores and bathers
who meet suddenly with little on,
and a generation later
they gurgle with stories
of family and bathing in the ocean
and of swimming very far out.

Wartime

1.
It fell to the dad –
after the last salvos,
after all the priests
had fled the town,
to baptize the infant child
and then hide him in high grass
near a muscular sprite
to provide against starvation,
shield against fire, war,
and the iron bands of closed borders.
The grasses betrayed nothing.

2.
The hidden child and his protector
have grown through the years,
one taller the other smaller.
Invisible, they're spared the views
of cities and towns burned and blistered.
Between the blasts and silences,
a measured time prevails,
filled with imaginings:
the bombs land as duds,
the sirens ring false alarms,
and the grasses part as they walk out.

Straus Park Memorial[2]

When the ship began its incline
at 11:40, on that cold April night
in the North Atlantic, Ida
and Isador descended together
first to their cabin – a hasty kiss,
a frightened embrace –
and then down further
into the fast-encircling sea.

They froze in the water
together and forever. Before
the slow slide into the deep,
she had declined the lifeboat
provided for the sick, the fragile,
women and children.

For them, the nautical disaster
was not a symbol or metaphor
for current disorder or loss,
not a request for sacrificial love or fame,
not an occurrence in the past.

---

[2] Straus Park (Broadway and 106th St. Manhattan) with its bronze statue "of a nymph gazing over a calm expanse of water," was built to memorialize Ida and Isidor Straus, who died together on the *Titanic*.- The memorial contains a passage from Second Samuel 1:23, "Lovely and pleasant were they in their lives and in their death they were not parted."

Wartime Blues

BLAST
The war – when we're lucky –
happens outside this room.
Safe inside, we suffer the usual:
the persistent headache,
the eternal sniffle,
the pictures on TV
of toddlers out there
holding the wheel.

BLAST
The locusts of Abaddon
form a cloud
over the front lines.
Angels of the Abyss
frown upon a Main Battle Tank
where the brain-dead driver,
scorched by the blaze,
stalls and then drives on.

BLAST
War now as in the past
troubles the living
to bury the dead.
The killing instinct
possessed even by the well-dressed,
asserts itself.
The wildfires of California are spreading,
and the earth quakes from China to the west.

Charlie's in Danger

Before the war Charlie studied the maps,
formations of troops, forward positions
and rocks to hide behind.

Run out of pushpins, he lowered the map
onto a table and made marks
only a few could follow.

There was noise on the radio
about the old maps becoming obsolete,
and then there was static.

From outside his window
he sees a million toy soldiers advancing
and a distant hand moving them

across an unmapped landscape
over cities, towns, open fields
and into a village square.

That hand is gloved,
while the other
snaps its fingers to a martial beat.

Folly

Fit armor on the chests of boys
let them play in the fray
with a good luck badge
pinned to their chests.
They step off the measure
they sing songs off key

> *cheer for an upward motion*
> *a bip the bop of zam*

Now here's a dentist
who treats infected teeth
with sticks of gum and
here's a doctor
famous on TV for his smile
and the wealth of his germs

> *cheer for an upward motion*
> *the flow into splendor*
> *a bip in the bop of zam*

Watch the forceps
in the hands of that toddler
about to deliver his sister
his posture's steady
despite the giggles
the grownups not yet old
tease the dying with forever

cheer for the upward motion,
the slip into splendor
the flow elevating the dross
a bip in the bop of zam

The Chief

> "History is a nightmare from which I am trying to awake"
> -James Joyce

1.
Without a Name

The Chief's name lit up the sky
and left it damaged,
but the sky stayed sky,
and the mountains too – mountains,
and the restless bodies of water
all remained indifferent
to the fabrications
of our grownup darling
who won the minds he won
by remaining a child
grown into a prankster
dressed in a scowl or a golden smile
that escapes all doubt.

At the rallies he thrills the fans;
they see and hear and feel
how he's been so unfairly hurt –
a martyr untied to any cause
or country.
Under the whine of his voice,
they embrace his grievances
and wear them like their own.
When the show ends,
they carry their thrills home,
itches in need of a claw.

2.
The Chief, Still Without a Name

is also without fabric.
Here's the question:
is this faker a phantom,
a specter spawning a spectacle
devoid of song or dance
or comedy, or is this a construction
out of deranged imaginations
in need of a catalyst,
or is this the fantasy of an adolescent frog
who's been stepped on by a nightmare
from which I'm trying to awake.

Cancel Culture

"He's known as Chile's Greatest Poet, But Feminists Say Pablo Neruda is Canceled"

Edison's bulb canceled the darkness
TV canceled radio – now an echo

The cyclone, signposts in its way,
cancelled the breezy day

Blacks canceled black-face
Bruce Lee canceled "slant-eye"

Militants canceled the talk of Covid
and other colors, hues and drawls

I canceled a trip to Sluggersville
where the score stayed tied

Cancel the conversation around rape
cancel the victim – cancel the wrong

Cancel *Lolita, 1984, Huck Finn …*
Cancel the defenders of books

Cancel the memory of '69
when nothing was canceled

Tidal Pools

They rest at the ocean's edge
ripple free,
while beneath the surface
barely visible intimate life
clings, crawls and thrives
within this façade of inaction.
The anemone, snails, barnacles, mussels,
limpets, periwinkles, sea stars,
chitons, sea urchins – and
all the filmy sea lettuces,
weeds, grasses --
their variegated natures quiver and stir.

Back on the surface
a sudden leaf or breeze alters the scene.
Thin waves canter to the margins,
each one fatter than the one before.
Soon the daily tide will disrupt
to deliver fresh nutrients
for the population:
plankton, and the minuscular flora,
all delicious edibles.
They flutter, as giant breakers
one after the other splash down –
a flood providing.
It's feeding time; all dine
beneath the oncoming shadow.

The Sea Speaks to the Sand

I've come to kiss you
old mud puddle–
while you hold back my flow,
banking me out to make me calm
and then new water
to fill a footprint.
My mind is muddy too
and always has been, but
it's with lunar intent
when I flood the continents.

At the same time – lapping upon your shore –
you're a favor, a harbor –
home free and famous for leisure.
I can settle down for a while,
kiss your skirts for a while,
dribble up by the bay.
What you see of me now
is just an edge of myself.

If I were so inclined,
I'd embrace this sandbar,
cradle each pebble,
each grain.
Oh, disappearing sand
and structures beyond,
one last wet kiss,
one last sloppy kiss
before the deluge.

Playing in Overtime

Survivor

Surely it was an error or a lucky punch
that let me slip through
to continue in this living room,
the best room on the planet,
when the others have left,
some few, years ago
some others, just lately.

They no longer know I'm here
in the room, or maybe,
possessed by magic,
some do know
and think my way,
feel into the corners
of this large room.

It cools a little
every time someone leaves.
All the coats, hats, scarves,
neatly hung in the closet,
are bored on their hangers,
devoid of utility.

So, I stick around
and envision my needs,
palpate my hunger,
photograph all I can,
find the music
that keeps me listening
and in touch with the players.
Out this plate glass window
beauties pass by,
a phoebe, a falling feather,
a postal worker with parcels,
boys and girls who vibrate
on the verdant lawn.
The past tense makes no sense.

Last Leaf

From my image on the pond,
I know my blush is deep,
my edges curl,
and my stem, though attached,
is drying. I'll soon be on your surface.

Tonight's predicted rainstorm
may sail me to your topmost edge.
Once that happens –
the inescapable small tumble –
we'll be a spectacle of color.

But I'll hang here a little longer.
It may not rain after all,
so, there's extra time
while you wait for me.

Come spring
I could be lingering still,
the last leaf upon the tree.

His November

Every inch forward upon the going on trail
is one inch closer to the go-no-further
signpost – where the trail meanders
to its terminal ledge.

A crowd of beasts – humans included –
is pressing close to the edge
with its sudden drop
into where

Pantoum for the Moment

To decry the day gone by scrubs the sheen off the now.
Challenged by slights, current and remembered,
I hide behind a bank of fog silvered by light,
and the neglected moment shivers from a chill.

My mind, challenged by current and remembered slights,
tries to spite the pain and staunch the fear,
while the moment, silver coated by chance, shivers from a chill.
The past – last week – retreats, a sad delinquent.

Spite the pain, staunch the fear that runs
across the brain with electric leaps and memory deletions.
The past escapes, unobserved and delinquent.
The future distracts from the moment's slippery climb.

The brain's electric leaps and random deletions,
sprout cityscapes of crisscrossed avenues out of town.
The future washes over the slippery climb to now.
To decry the day gone by dulls the sheen of today.

Companion

It was but a small spike
that pierced and then settled
in the shallows of my gut.
This did not pain me greatly,
nor did it make me sing.
Happily, last week,
the spike didn't move
while I was beset by the giggles.
Any wriggling
would have torn my insides out.
So, I didn't move, played dead,
and the pain pretended to be gone
and let me bask in the shade for a while.

Now, the sticking feeling visits regularly
no matter what space or room
where I might hide the body.
It can turn hostile or glum.
Still, friends call or come to witness
the pain's amazing dexterity
as it shifts, hitting all the right zones
of interest. Are you a sharpy,
or is your presence hard-nosed dull?
You'll last as long as you will
as will I.

A Fluky Fall

A bar of soap – more likely a large sliver
slipped out of his grasp
onto the shower floor.
He then slid and cracked his noggin;
blood went down the drain.

This was his fabulous fall, –
the end to all wars.
Now forever he's out of the weather.
No further anticipations
of future emendations
of gripes over this or that,
never another paper cut,
hiccup, heart palpitation,
swerving rides to the hospital.

He'll miss the storms, the pallid migrations,
ghosts leaving ghost towns,
the silence of church bells,
and best of all/ and worst of all
the grimace on his loves' faces
when they hear the news.

Penultimate Words

This man, near to his end,
glimpses the mound up ahead
and cries out: "All this goes with me —
the clean suit they'll dress the thing in
pockets empty of cash
the botched memory
the failure to spell in any language
the chipped tooth just off center
the deformed arthritic fourth finger
on the left hand that won't fist
the fear of losing gold
and silver fillings too.
I take them with me
along with the fear of falling.
Shovel fresh soil on the lot,
bury the scorn / the unreason
and the idea of dates in time –
shove them well under.
Entomb the vain rational.

He said all this and
put his feet up on the table.

Speedo

Monday, he awoke early.
Amazed by the mirror
he saw himself as wing-footed Mercury
the first around the block
sipping coffee on the fly
wiping a sleeve across his godly mouth.

He sensed Tuesday in his stride
checked the clock for Wednesday
dove into a deep minute's doze
before waking in time to jump up and
dance around with Thursday.
Friday was just as fleeting just as frantic.

At noon, he checked a timepiece
and midnight whispered "easy."
That was a swift week he thought
then his inner guide beckoned softly
moderate your pace, relax your time.

With the weekend everything changed.
He floated on a slow gin fizz
relaxed with company
conversational chatter
Chopin in the air.

The Speed of a Bullet

*"The light at the end of the tunnel
is an oncoming train"*

is a phrase found
in the public domain;
and the light gets brighter
as the train comes closer
and louder –

A bullet named Time
heads towards Death
but Death ducks, straightens up,
brushes off the perennial dust
and kills Time – temporarily.

Time's remnants march on.
Might this line of thought
be a waste of time?

An Escape

It stepped out of its shadow,
grinned, and spit a poison
in my direction.
I ducked, ran to mother,
whispered words into her ear –
"tell it that I,
the fruit of your loins,
the light of your maturity,
am out of town
and will not be around anytime soon."
She did.

It sprouted wings, left the area
and made like a helicopter
dipping down, circling, rising,
searching all the vicinities
for someone else – a monkey even –
or a boy having an ice cream cone.

The monkey escaped,
safe into its mother's arms.
The old man sitting in a corner is still
too visible. It already tastes him.
It licks its chops around the clock.
I'm on my way into another zone
along with mother and her wisdom.
There looms the universal risk
of outlasting the mother.

Recollection
> *For Marvin Cohen*

It's been said
that nothing's remembered
that hasn't already happened.
So, early on,
I squeezed out of my nappy,
bent the bars of the crib,
and crawled into action,
a maker of memories.

I remember the shape of the rooms
I crawled into and the furnishings,
the fixtures, the works of art,
who walked in,
who walked out
and who stayed.

I remember their faces around the table
but no longer the topics or the names.
My mind is a sieve.
Yet all that happened did happen:
the flirtations, the couplings
and the folds in the fabric,
entire episodes.

First Responder

Sometimes I rush like a first responder
to the silvered shards of my memories
stacked like poker chips.
I hurry should one, two or a few slip away
to join the other forgotten faces
and lost moments.

The pile, after all these years, is large.
From one shard, father calls to scold me,
from another, mother holds my hand
while I swim – knowing my fear of water.
My uncles, fresh from the war
tell me stories I cannot understand.

It's my job to save the moments
and keep them alive,
perform triage on my memories
and greet them warmly on their return.
I'm a first responder
and the last.

Grim Reaper

This phenomenon
nicknamed Skull by some,
Star by others (twinkle twinkle),
can't be reached
by phone, mail, email,
or TikTok toe.
A stay-away gesture –
not now – later please –
has failed so far.

When he – the gendered
motha-hubba –
makes his regular rounds,
I wonder out loud
if he's missed someone &
how long can this go on &
if & where I'm headed next.

Our animal friends,
our multitudinous brethren,
bereft of mythologies,
simply flinch, dash
or expire.

As of Late, It's Still Early

Still early today, the time-measurers agree.
They sense the merits of slowdown,
and soon they crouch, then crawl on all fours –
joyous beasts with ideas to serve up for tomorrow.

They are the disheveled ones, brilliant,
who thrash about in the underbrush
tangled within the brambles and burrs –
scrambling away in their time.

Soon they'll climb the majestic branches
beyond the threatening thorns.
They'll perch above the late comers
who shilly-shallied the day away.

But it's not even noon!
They are taking pictures,
freezing each millisecond.
This day goes on till lights out.

The Race

They say – and I don't quarrel –
Time flies;
so, at a venerable age,
prone to fabrication,
I went into training:
Long distance runs
over the tended paths
of North South Park
followed by quarter-mile sprints,
and after a break,
for liniment and recovery,
a 100-yard dash.

In the evening – after a hurried bite,
a sip of something cold,
and a meditative pause,
I head for the bike
and peddle against resistance
the machine's and my own.

My stopwatch is hot.
I've an hour's lead on Time,
but don't know how near the finish line.
I'm resigned – when over my shoulder
I see that fleeting thing, Time, go by
With just enough time to look my way.

"Hereafter"
>	*for Philip Appleman*

"Man that is born of woman is of few days and full of trouble. He comes like a flower and is cut down. He flees also like a shadow and continues not."
Job 14:1-2

After, as in hereafter, annuls the here,
though it may be apt when prefaced by ever.
With ever after the heart pumps promise,
whereas hereafter spins on a pin.

The word confounds the senses
unmoored from the rational,
tethered to the sublime:
"until we meet again ...."

The ghosts approach the gates,
some pull themselves up and over,
some just sail beyond
and may achieve afterness,

while those of us still here
nevertheless, glance forward.

Lost and Found

I was lost in time
when autumn rhymed
with a glass of wine

and stayed the day past twilight.

Lost in the woods
troubled by the shoulds
that really were coulds

all the way to the thickets.

Lost in the room
beset by gloom
reversed by a burst of sudden bloom

that set the stage for brightness.

Found myself in a groove
ready to move
the levers of thought to improve

what's left of the day.

About the Author

Barry Wallenstein is the author of twelve collections of poetry, the most recent being *Odd Men Out (or In)* [Xanadu Press, 2025], *It's About Time* [New York Quarterly Books, 2022] and *Time on the Move* [Xanadu Press, 2020]. His poetry has appeared in over 100 journals, including *Ploughshares, The Nation, American Poetry Review* and *Manhattan Review*. A special interest is his presentation of poetry readings in collaboration with jazz. He has made twelve recordings of his poetry with jazz, the most recent being *Lisbon Sunrise* (2022) and *Lisbon Sunset* (2018).

Barry is Emeritus Professor of Literature and Creative Writing at the City University of New York and an editor of the journal, *American Book Review,* and advisory editor of *BigCityLit*. Since retiring from CUNY, he's been part of the faculty at the Center for Learning and Living, a continuing ed program for seniors.

www.ingramcontent.com/pod-product-compliance
Lightning Source LLC
Chambersburg PA
CBHW061810070526
44586CB00024B/2790